Christmas at Home

Holiday Cookies & Desserts

compiled by
Ellyn Sanna

BARBOUR
PUBLISHING, INC.
Uhrichsville, Ohio

© MCMXCIX by Barbour Publishing, Inc.

ISBN 1-57748-594-7

Published by Barbour Publishing, Inc., P.O. Box 719, Uhrichsville, Ohio 44683
http://www.barbourbooks.com

 Member of the
Evangelical Christian
Publishers Association

Printed in Canada

Something about Christmas makes even the least domestic of us want to get out the mixing bowls and flour and spices. The warm fragrance of cinnamon and sugar and vanilla fills our homes, reminding us of Christmases when we were small and our mothers were the ones doing the baking. As we fill our ovens with trays of sweet confection, we relive one of the best parts of our childhood.

And as plate after plate is filled with cookies, we have bounty to pass on to our friends and neighbors and coworkers, a delicious Christmas greeting to share.

$\mathcal{A}$s you bake this year, remember—
each cookie and cake honors the birthday of Jesus,
the Son of God and the Son of man.

Cookie
Recipes

Springerle

(Christmas Aniseed Cookies)

4 eggs
2 cups sugar
1 tsp aniseed or anise extract
4 ¼ cups flour
1 tsp baking soda

Beat eggs until fluffy, then add sugar a little at a time until mixture is thick (about 10 minutes with mixer). Beat in aniseed. Sift flour and baking soda together and beat into egg mixture a little at a time. Knead dough until smooth, working in flour if the dough is sticky. Chill for 2 hours.

Roll out dough on a floured surface to a ½-inch thickness. Flour springerle mold or rolling pin and press firmly into dough. Cut cookies into 1 ½-inch squares and arrange on a lined cookie sheet. Dry at room temperature for about a day, then bake at 300°F for 30 minutes until bottoms are golden. Store in airtight container. Makes about 40 cookies.

Cranberry Almond Shortbread Thumbprints

1 cup butter or margarine, softened
⅔ cup sugar
½ tsp almond extract
2 cups flour

FILLING
⅓ cup red plum jam
¼ cup cranberries

Beat butter, sugar, and almond extract together at medium speed for 1 to 2 minutes until creamy. Reduce speed and beat in flour. Form dough into 1-inch balls and place on an ungreased cookie sheet, 2 inches apart. Press thumb into the center of each cookie to make an indentation. Combine jam and cranberries. Put about ¼ tsp of mixture into the center of each cookie. Bake at 350°F for 14 to 18 minutes, until edges are light brown. Makes about 3 ½ dozen cookies.

Snowtime Ginger Cookies

1 ¼ cups sugar
1 cup butter or margarine, softened
1 egg
3 tbsp dark corn syrup
1 tsp vanilla
3 cups flour
1 ½ tsp baking soda
2 tsp cinnamon
1 tsp ginger
¼ tsp salt
¼ tsp cloves

Mix sugar and butter at medium speed for 1 to 2 minutes until well mixed. Beat in egg, corn syrup, and vanilla for another 1 to 2 minutes. Reduce speed and add flour, baking soda, cinnamon, ginger, salt, and cloves. Divide dough into three parts and shape each part into a ball, then flatten balls to ½ inch. Wrap dough in plastic wrap and refrigerate for 1 to 2 hours. Roll out dough to ⅛ inch, one-third at a time. Cut with 2- to 3-inch cookie cutters and place on an ungreased cookie sheet, one inch apart. Bake for 5 to 7 minutes at 375°F. Makes about 7 dozen cookies.

Candy Cane Twists

1 ½ cups powdered sugar
1 ¼ cups butter or margarine, softened
1 egg
1 tsp peppermint extract
1 tsp vanilla
2 ¾ cups flour
¼ tsp salt
⅓ cup finely crushed candy canes,
   or peppermint candy
¼ tsp red food coloring

Beat powdered sugar, butter, egg, peppermint extract, and vanilla together at medium speed until creamy. Reduce speed and add flour and salt. Divide dough in half. Stir candy into one half of the dough and beat food coloring into the other half. For each cookie, roll 1 tsp of each dough into a 4-inch long rope. Place ropes beside each other and twist them together. Place on an ungreased cookie sheet and curve one end of cookie to make the shape of a candy cane. Bake at 350°F for 10 to 12 minutes. Makes about 4 ½ dozen cookies.

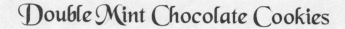

Double Mint Chocolate Cookies

BATTER
1 cup sugar
½ cup cocoa
1 egg
½ cup butter or margarine, softened
½ tsp vanilla
2 cups flour
1 tsp baking soda
1 tsp baking powder
¼ tsp salt
½ cup buttermilk
½ cup water

FROSTING
2 cups powdered sugar
1 to 2 tbsp milk
½ tsp salt
½ cup butter or margarine, softened
1 tsp vanilla
¼ tsp mint extract
¼ cup crushed peppermint candy

Mix sugar, cocoa, butter, egg, and vanilla at medium speed until well mixed. At reduced speed, add flour, baking soda, baking powder, and salt a little at a time. Alternately add buttermilk and water. Drop dough by rounded teaspoons onto a greased cookie sheet, 2 inches apart. Bake at 400°F for 7 to 9 minutes.

Cool completely. Combine all frosting ingredients except candy. Beat until creamy. Spread about 1 tbsp of frosting on top of each cookie and sprinkle with crushed candy. Makes about 4 dozen cookies.

Chocolate
Coffee Cookies

1 ⅔ cups sugar
⅔ cup butter or margarine, softened
⅓ plus ¼ cup brewed coffee, cooled
2 eggs
2 (1-ounce) squares unsweetened baking
    chocolate, melted
2 tsp vanilla
2 ¾ cups flour
2 tsp baking powder
¾ tsp salt
¼ tsp cinnamon

FROSTING
3 tbsp butter or margarine, softened
3 cups powdered sugar
5 to 6 tbsp brewed coffee, cooled
chocolate chips, melted (optional)

Combine sugar, butter, coffee, eggs, melted chocolate, and vanilla. Beat at medium speed until creamy. Reduce speed and add flour, baking powder, salt, and cinnamon. Drop by rounded teaspoons onto an ungreased cookie sheet, 2 inches apart. Bake at 350°F for 8 to 12 minutes. Remove from cookie sheets and cool completely. Combine all frosting ingredients except coffee. Beat at low speed, adding enough coffee to bring frosting to desired spreading consistency. Frost cookies and if desired, drizzle with melted chocolate chips. Makes about 5 dozen cookies.

Candy Window Cookies

¾ cup sugar
1 cup butter or margarine, softened
1 (3-ounce) package cream cheese, softened
1 egg
1 tsp vanilla
3 cups flour

DECORATIONS
fruit-flavored hard candy, finely crushed
decorator sugars and candies

Combine all cookie ingredients except flour. Beat at medium speed until creamy. Reduce speed and add flour, beating just until mixed. Divide dough into two parts. Cover and refrigerate for 2 hours, or overnight. Roll out one half of the dough into a 15 x 10-inch rectangle. Cut dough into 20 rectangles with a knife or pastry wheel. Cut small shapes in the center of each rectangle with tiny cookie cutters, hors d'oeuvre cutters, or a knife. Save cutout shapes. Place cookies on a foil-lined cookie sheet. Fill cutout holes evenly with crushed candy. Roll out second half of dough in the same way and cut into rectangles. Put cutout shapes on top of cookies. Sprinkle with decorator sugars or candies, if desired. Bake at 325°F for 7 to 9 minutes. Makes about 3 dozen cookies.

Holiday
Candy Cookie Bites

1 ⅓ cups packed brown sugar
⅔ cup butter or margarine, softened
⅓ cup peanut butter
2 eggs
2 tsp vanilla
1 cup flour
1 tsp baking powder
½ tsp baking soda
2 ½ cups quick-cooking oats
1 (10-ounce) package red and green
   candy-coated chocolate pieces
1 cup vanilla chips

Mix brown sugar, butter, and peanut butter at medium speed. Beat in eggs and vanilla. Reduce speed and add flour, baking powder, and baking soda. By hand, stir in oats, candy pieces, and vanilla chips. Line miniature muffin pans with paper liners. Drop heaping teaspoons of dough into liners. Bake at 350°F for 15 to 17 minutes. Makes about 6 dozen cookies.

Buttery Jam Tarts

2 ½ cups flour
½ cup sugar
⅔ cup butter or margarine, softened
¼ tsp baking soda
¼ tsp salt
2 tbsp milk
1 egg
1 tsp almond extract
½ cup raspberry preserves

At low speed, beat together all ingredients except raspberry preserves. Roll out dough on a floured surface, half at a time. Refrigerate remaining dough. Roll dough to 1/8-inch thickness and cut with a 2 1/2-inch round cookie cutter. Place half the cookies on a greased cookie sheet, 2 inches apart. Put 1 tsp preserves on top of each cookie. Make a small x in the remaining cookies, or else cut a hole in them with a little cookie cutter. Place these cookies on top of the preserves, pressing the edges together with a fork. Bake at 350°F for 12 to 15 minutes. Makes about 2 dozen cookies.

Scandinavian Kringla

3 ⅓ cups flour
1 tsp baking powder
½ tsp baking soda
¼ tsp salt
¾ cup sugar

½ cup butter or margarine,
    softened
2 eggs
2 tsp vanilla
⅔ cup buttermilk

EGG WASH
1 egg

1 tbsp water

Beat together sugar and butter at medium speed until creamy. Beat in eggs and vanilla. Reduce speed and add flour, baking powder, baking soda, and salt alternately with buttermilk, beating well after each addition. Cover and refrigerate for 4 hours, or overnight. Mix ingredients of Sweet Raspberry Butter (on next page).

SWEET RASPBERRY BUTTER FOR KRINGLA
1 cup butter or margarine, softened
¼ cup raspberry jam
¼ tsp cinnamon

TOPPING
2 tbsp powdered sugar
1 tsp cinnamon

Cover and store in the refrigerator. Flour hands and shape dough into 1-inch balls. Roll each ball into a 10-inch long rope on a floured surface. Place each rope on an ungreased cookie sheet in a U-shape, crossing the ends to form a pretzel shape. Brush the cookies with the egg wash mixture. Bake at 350°F for 9 to 12 minutes. Cool completely. Just before serving, sprinkle topping mixture over Kringla. Serve with Sweet Raspberry Butter. Makes about 4 dozen cookies.

Stamped Ginger Cookies

1 cup butter or margarine, softened
⅔ cup powdered sugar
1 tsp vanilla
2 cups flour
½ tsp ground ginger
¼ tsp salt
¼ cup finely chopped crystallized ginger

Mix butter, powdered sugar, and vanilla at medium speed until creamy. Reduce speed and add flour, ground ginger, and salt. Stir in crystallized ginger by hand. Shape dough into 1-inch balls and place on an ungreased cookie sheet, 2 inches apart. Flatten balls to ¼ inch with a 2-inch cookie stamp. Bake at 325°F for 12 to 15 minutes. Makes about 3 ½ dozen cookies.

Chocolate Holiday Cookies

⅔ cup powdered sugar
½ cup butter or margarine, softened
½ tsp vanilla

1 cup flour
2 tbsp cocoa
⅛ tsp salt

ICING
1 ¼ cups powdered sugar
1 tbsp meringue powder

2 tbsp warm water
¼ tsp cream of tartar

Beat together powdered sugar, butter, and vanilla at medium speed. Reduce speed and add flour, cocoa, and salt. Divide dough in half. One half at a time, place dough between sheets of lightly floured waxed paper and roll out to $1/8$-inch thickness, refrigerating remaining half. Remove paper and cut with 2- to 2 ½-inch cookie cutters. Place on an ungreased cookie sheet. Bake at 325°F for 14 to 18 minutes.

Combine icing ingredients and beat at low speed until moistened. Increase speed and beat until stiff and glossy. Add more warm water if icing becomes too stiff. Cover with damp paper towel until ready to use. Cool cookies completely before decorating with icing as desired. Makes about 2 dozen cookies.

Nutmeg Butterfingers

1 cup butter or margarine,
   softened
¾ cup sugar
1 egg

2 tsp vanilla
3 cups flour
¾ tsp nutmeg

FROSTING
2 cups powdered sugar
⅓ cup butter or margarine,
   softened
1 tbsp nutmeg

1 tsp vanilla
2 tsp rum-flavored
   extract, if desired

Mix butter and sugar at medium speed until creamy. Add egg and vanilla. Reduce speed and add flour and nutmeg. Form dough into 3 ½-inch fingers and place on a greased cookie sheet. Bake at 350°F for 13 to 15 minutes. Beat together all frosting ingredients. Spread frosting on cooled cookies. Sprinkle lightly with nutmeg. Makes about 6 dozen cookies.

Double Delights

1 cup sugar
¾ cup butter or margarine, softened
1 egg
2 tsp vanilla
2 ¼ cups flour
1 tsp baking powder
¼ tsp salt
2 (1-ounce) squares unsweetened
    baking chocolate, melted

Beat sugar and butter together at medium speed until creamy. Add egg and vanilla. Reduce speed and add flour, baking powder, and salt. Divide dough into two parts. Wrap half the dough in waxed paper. Add melted chocolate to remaining half and beat at low speed until just mixed. Wrap chocolate dough in waxed paper. Refrigerate both halves for at least an hour. Shape rounded teaspoons of dough into desired shapes, using both doughs. Place on an ungreased cookie sheet, 1 inch apart. Bake at 375°F for 7 to 8 minutes. Decorate as desired after cooling. Makes about 3 dozen cookies.

Chocolate Chip Thumbprints

½ cup packed brown sugar
½ cup butter or margarine,
   softened
1 tsp vanilla
½ tsp salt
1 cup flour

¼ cup mini semisweet
   chocolate chips
2 tbsp milk
powdered sugar

FILLING

¾ cup mini semisweet chocolate chips
1 tbsp shortening
2 tbsp white corn syrup

1 tsp water
1 tsp vanilla

At medium speed, beat together brown sugar, butter, vanilla, and salt. Reduce speed and mix in flour, chocolate chips, and milk. Form dough into 1-inch balls. Place balls on an ungreased cookie sheet, 1 inch apart. Press thumb into each cookie to make an indentation. Bake at 375°F for 10 to 12 minutes. If necessary, make indentation again. Cool completely, then sprinkle with powdered sugar. For filling: Melt chocolate chips together with shortening over low heat. Stir occasionally. Cool slightly, then stir in corn syrup, water, and vanilla. Spoon about 1 tsp of filling into each cookie indentation. Makes about 2 dozen cookies.

Cinnamon Blossoms

1 cup butter or margarine, softened
¾ cup sugar
1 egg yolk
1 tsp vanilla
2 cups flour
1 ½ tsp cinnamon
¼ tsp salt
60 mini chocolate kisses

Combine butter, sugar, egg yolk, and vanilla, beating on medium speed until creamy. Reduce speed and add flour, cinnamon, and salt. Fill cookie press with dough. Press dough onto an ungreased cookie sheet, 1 inch apart. Bake at 375°F for 8 to 11 minutes. As soon as cookies are removed from the oven, place 1 chocolate in the center of each. Makes 5 dozen cookies.

Orange Pistachio
Butter Balls

1 cup butter or margarine, softened
½ cup powdered sugar
2 cups flour
1 cup finely chopped, salted pistachio nuts
2 tsp grated orange peel
2 tsp vanilla
powdered sugar

Mix butter and powdered sugar at medium speed until creamy. Reduce speed and add flour, nuts, orange peel, and vanilla. Form dough into 1-inch balls. Place balls on an ungreased cookie sheet, 1 inch apart. Bake at 350°F for 9 to 11 minutes. Roll cookies in powdered sugar while still warm and again after being cooled. Makes about 5 dozen cookies.

Scottish Shortbread

1 ¾ cups flour
¾ cup powdered sugar
½ cup cake flour

1 cup butter or margarine,
    softened
½ tsp sugar

TOPPING
1 tbsp sugar

⅛ tsp cinnamon

Combine all shortbread ingredients and stir together with a fork to make a soft dough. Press dough into the bottom of 2 (9-inch) shortbread molds and prick all over with a fork. Bake at 350°F for 20 to 30 minutes. Cool for about 10 minutes, then loosen edges with a knife and invert onto a wooden board. Stir together topping ingredients and sprinkle over shortbread. Cut into wedges. Makes about 16 servings.

Angel Cookies

1 cup sugar
1 cup butter or margarine,
  softened
1 egg
1 tsp vanilla
½ tsp almond extract

2 cups flour
½ tsp baking soda
½ tsp cream of tartar
¼ tsp salt
water
sugar

Beat together sugar and butter at medium speed until creamy. Add egg, vanilla, and almond extract, beating well. Reduce speed and add flour, baking soda, cream of tartar, and salt. Shape dough into 1-inch balls. Dip the top of each ball into water, then into sugar. Place the balls on an ungreased cookie sheet, 2 inches apart. Bake at 375°F for 7 to 9 minutes. Makes about 3 dozen cookies.

Spritz Surprise Cookies

1 cup butter or margarine,
  softened
⅔ cup sugar

2 ¼ cups flour
1 tbsp vanilla
1 egg

1 (8-ounce) package individually wrapped, assorted miniature chocolate bars (¼-ounce each)

Mix butter, sugar, egg, and vanilla at medium speed until creamy. Reduce speed and add flour. Fill cookie press with dough and attach ribbon template. Press half the dough onto ungreased cookie sheets in 14 ½-inch long ribbons. Break chocolate bars into ¾- to 1-inch pieces and place on strips of dough, ½-inch apart. Press remaining dough in ribbons over candy. Mark dough between chocolate pieces with a table knife. Bake at 375°F for 10 to 15 minutes. While cookies are still warm, cut or break them apart at marks. Makes about 4 ½ dozen cookies.

Eggnog Glazed Spritz Cookies

1 cup butter or margarine, softened
⅔ cup sugar
1 egg

1 tbsp vanilla
2 ¼ cups flour
1 tsp nutmeg

GLAZE
1 cup powdered sugar
¼ cup butter or margarine,
  melted

¼ tsp rum-flavored
  extract
1 to 2 tbsp hot water

Beat together butter, sugar, egg, and vanilla at medium speed until creamy. Reduce speed and add flour and nutmeg. Fill cookie press with dough and press cookies out onto an un-greased cookie sheet, 1 inch apart. Bake at 375°F for 6 to 10 minutes. Stir together glaze ingredients, using enough hot water for desired consistency. While cookies are still warm, brush their tops with glaze. Makes about 4 dozen cookies.

Spicy Cardamom Crisps

1 ⅓ cups sugar
1 cup butter or margarine,
  softened
1 egg
2 tbsp dark corn syrup
1 tbsp water

1 tsp vanilla
3 cups flour
1 ½ tsp baking soda
2 tsp cardamom
½ tsp cinnamon
sliced almonds

Beat together sugar and butter at medium speed until creamy. Add egg, corn syrup, water, and vanilla, beating well. Reduce speed and beat in all remaining ingredients except the almonds. Divide the dough into three parts. Shape each third into a ½-inch thick square. Wrap each square in plastic wrap and refrigerate for 1 to 2 hours. Roll out dough, one third at a time, on a lightly floured surface, forming a 12 x 10-inch rectangle. Cut into 2-inch squares using a knife or pastry cutter. Cut squares in half diagonally to form triangles. Place triangles on an ungreased cookie sheet, 1 inch apart. Press almonds into the center of each cookie. Bake at 375°F for 7 to 9 minutes. Makes about 7 ½ dozen cookies.

Lemon Meltaways

1 ¼ cups flour
½ cup cornstarch
⅓ cup powdered sugar
¾ cup butter or margarine, softened
1 tsp grated lemon peel
1 tbsp lemon juice

FROSTING
¾ cup powdered sugar
¼ cup butter or margarine, softened
1 tsp grated lemon peel
1 tsp lemon juice

Beat together all cookie ingredients at low speed until well mixed. Divide dough in half, forming each half into an 8 x 1-inch roll. Wrap the rolls of dough in plastic wrap and refrigerate for 1 to 2 hours. Cut dough into ¼-inch slices and place on a cookie sheet, 2 inches apart. Bake at 350°F for 8 to 12 minutes.

Beat together all frosting ingredients at medium speed until fluffy. Frost the cookies after they have cooled completely. Makes about 4 dozen cookies.

Mocha Toffee Crescents

1 tsp instant espresso granules
1 tbsp warm water
1 cup butter or margarine, softened
⅔ cup powdered sugar
2 cups flour
¼ tsp salt
½ cup toffee chips

Dissolve espresso granules in warm water. Combine espresso mixture with butter and powdered sugar, beating at medium speed until creamy. Reduce speed and add flour and salt. Stir in toffee chips by hand. Shape teaspoons of dough into crescents. Place crescents on an ungreased cookie sheet, 1 inch apart. Bake at 325°F for 13 to 17 minutes. If desired, roll cookies in powdered sugar or dip them in a mixture of ½ cup melted semi-sweet chocolate chips and 2 tsp shortening. Makes about 3 ½ dozen cookies.

Norwegian Cookies

1 ⅓ cups sugar
1 cup butter or margarine,
  softened
2 eggs
1 (12-ounce) package semisweet chocolate chips (2 cups)

1 tsp vanilla
3 cups flour
1 tsp baking powder

TOPPING
3 tbsp sugar

¾ tsp cinnamon

Mix sugar and butter together at medium speed until creamy. Beat in eggs and vanilla. Reduce speed and add flour and baking powder. Stir in chocolate chips by hand. Divide dough in half on a lightly floured surface. Divide each half into thirds and shape each of the parts into a 10-inch roll. Place 2 rolls per ungreased cookie sheet, at least 2 inches apart. Flatten each roll with a moistened fork to about ½ inch thick. Combine sugar and cinnamon and sprinkle about 1 ½ tsp of mixture on each roll. Bake at 350°F for 13 to 15 minutes. Slice diagonally into 1-inch strips while still warm. Makes about 6 dozen cookies.

Brownie Christmas Trees

   1 (19.8 to 21.5-ounce) package plain brownie mix
   ½ cup butter or margarine, melted

FROSTING
3 cups powdered sugar
½ cup butter or margarine, softened
1 tsp vanilla
3 to 4 tbsp milk
3 to 4 drops green food coloring
2 to 3 tbsp miniature candy-coated chocolate pieces
28 (1- to 1 ½-inch) pretzel rod pieces

Prepare brownie mix according to package directions except substitute melted butter for oil. Pour batter into a 13 x 9-inch baking pan, lined with greased foil. Bake at 350°F for 30 to 33 minutes. Cool. Combine powdered sugar, butter, vanilla, and enough milk for desired consistency. Add food coloring. Remove brownie from pan and remove foil. When completely cool, frost. Cut brownie into 4 (3-inch) rows. Cut each row into seven triangles. Press chocolate pieces into frosting. Insert pretzel into one side for a tree trunk. Makes 28 trees.

Almond Butter Cookies

1 cup butter or margarine
¾ cup sugar
1 tsp almond extract

2 cups flour
½ tsp baking powder
¼ tsp salt

GLAZE
½ cup semisweet chocolate chips
2 tsp shortening

Beat together butter, sugar, and almond extract on medium speed. Reduce speed and add flour, baking powder, and salt. Form rounded teaspoons of dough into 1-inch balls. Place balls on an ungreased cookie sheet, 2 inches apart. With the bottom of buttered glass dipped in sugar, flatten balls to ¼ inch thick.

Bake at 400°F for 6 to 8 minutes. Melt chocolate chips and shortening together over low heat, stirring until smooth. Drizzle onto cooled cookies. Makes about 5 dozen cookies.

Chocolate-Dipped Citrus Ribbons

1 cup butter or margarine,
  softened
⅔ cup sugar
1 egg

1 tbsp orange juice
1 ½ tsp grated orange peel
½ tsp vanilla
2 ½ cups flour

CHOCOLATE DIP
1 cup vanilla milk chips
1 cup semisweet chocolate chips

2 tbsp shortening

At medium speed, beat together all cookie ingredients except flour. Reduce speed and mix in flour. Fill cookie press with dough and attach the ribbon template. Press dough in long continuous strips onto cookie sheet. Mark dough with a table knife every 3 inches. Bake at 350°F for 7 to 9 minutes. Cut or break cookies apart at marks. Cool completely. Melt vanilla milk chips with 1 tbsp shortening over low heat, stirring until smooth. Do the same for the chocolate chips and the remaining shortening. Pour melted mixtures side by side onto a plate and swirl together with a knife to marble. Dip one end of each cookie into marbled mixture. Makes about 6 ½ dozen cookies.

Holiday Cookie Slices

1 cup sugar
1 cup butter or margarine,
  softened
1 egg
2 tsp vanilla

2 ¼ cups flour
¼ tsp baking powder
¼ tsp salt
food coloring

Mix together sugar, butter, egg, and vanilla at medium speed until creamy. Reduce speed and add flour, baking powder, and salt. Form half the dough into a 6 x 2 ½-inch roll. Add food coloring to remaining dough and shape into a similar roll. Wrap both rolls in plastic wrap and refrigerate 3 hours, or overnight. Cut each roll into ¼-inch slices. Cut out the center of each cookie with 1- to 1 ½-inch cookie cutters. Place the cutout sections of the colored slices into the centers of the plain slices and vice versa. Place cookies on an ungreased cookie sheet. Bake at 375°F for 7 to 10 minutes. Makes about 4 dozen cookies.

Paintbrush Sugar Cookies

1 cup powdered sugar
1 cup butter or margarine,
  softened
2 egg yolks

1 tsp vanilla
2 ¼ cups flour
¼ tsp salt

EGG YOLK PAINT
1 egg yolk
assorted food coloring

¼ tsp water

Beat together powdered sugar and butter at medium speed until creamy. Beat in egg yolks and vanilla. Reduce speed and add flour and salt. Divide the dough into 2 balls and flatten each ball to ½ inch thick. Wrap both halves in plastic wrap and refrigerate for about 1 hour. Combine egg yolk and water and pour mixture into several cups. Stir a different color of food coloring into each cup. Cover until use. Roll out dough, half at a time, on a lightly floured surface. When dough is ⅛ inch thick, cut with 2 ½-inch cookie cutters and place cookies on an ungreased cookie sheet, 2 inches apart. With a small paintbrush, paint desired designs on cookies with egg yolk paint. Bake at 375°F for 5 to 8 minutes. Makes about 5 ½ dozen cookies.

Cranberry Chocolate Chip Cookies

1 cup butter or margarine,
  softened
¾ cup packed brown sugar
½ cup sugar
2 eggs
1 cup sweetened dried cranberries
1 (12-ounce) package chocolate chips

2 tsp vanilla
2 ½ cups flour
1 tsp baking soda
½ tsp salt

Mix together butter, brown sugar, sugar, eggs, and vanilla at medium speed. Reduce speed and add flour, baking soda, and salt. Stir in cranberries and chocolate chips by hand. Drop dough onto an ungreased cookie sheet by rounded teaspoons, 2 inches apart. Bake at 350°F for 10 to 12 minutes. Makes about 5 dozen cookies.

Chocolate Mint Wafers

1 (10-ounce) package vanilla-flavored candy coating
¼ tsp mint extract
2 to 3 drops green food coloring
1 (9-ounce) package chocolate wafers
¾ cup mint semisweet chocolate chips
1 tsp shortening

Melt vanilla candy coating over low heat. Remove from heat and add mint extract and food coloring, stirring well. Dip chocolate wafers halfway into melted coating. Place wafers on waxed, paper-lined cookie sheets. Melt mint chips and shortening over low heat, stirring until smooth. Drizzle melted chocolate over dipped wafers with a spoon. Allow chocolate to harden. Makes about 2 dozen cookies.

Hazelnut Lace Wafers

¼ cup sugar
¼ cup butter or margarine
3 tbsp dark corn syrup
1 (2-ounce) package hazelnuts, toasted, finely chopped (½ cup)

¼ tsp vanilla
½ cup flour

Combine sugar, butter, and corn syrup in a 1-quart sauce-pan. Stirring constantly, cook over medium heat until mixture comes to a boil. Remove from heat and stir in vanilla. Mix together flour and nuts and gradually add mixture to sugar mixture. Stir well after each addition. Drop dough onto an ungreased cookie sheet by rounded teaspoons, 3 inches apart. Bake at 350°F for 6 to 8 minutes. While still warm, press cookies around a spoon to form a cone shape.

White Chocolate Chunk Cookies

1 cup butter or margarine,
  softened
½ cup packed brown sugar
2 eggs
2 tsp vanilla

2 cups flour
1 tsp salt
¾ tsp baking soda
3 cups rolled oats
1 (12-ounce) package
  vanilla milk chips

Beat together butter and sugar at medium speed until creamy. Mix in eggs and vanilla. Reduce speed and add flour, salt, and baking soda. Stir in oats and vanilla chips by hand. Drop dough onto an ungreased cookie sheet by rounded teaspoons. Bake at 350°F for 10 to 12 minutes. Makes about 3 dozen cookies.

Vanilla and Chocolate Biscotti

2 cups flour
½ cup toasted walnuts,
  finely chopped
½ tsp baking powder
½ tsp baking soda
¼ tsp salt

1 cup sugar
¼ cup butter or margarine,
  softened
2 eggs
2 tsp vanilla
1 (1-ounce) square
  unsweetened chocolate,
  melted, cooled

DRIZZLE
¼ cup semisweet
  chocolate chips

¼ cup vanilla milk chips
2 tsp shortening

76

Mix sugar and butter at medium speed. Add eggs and vanilla. Reduce speed and add flour, walnuts, baking powder, baking soda, and salt. Remove half dough and add melted chocolate to remaining half. Divide both chocolate and white doughs into half. Roll each part into a 6-inch log. Place 1 chocolate log on top of 1 white log and roll together to form a roll 10 x 1 ½ inches. Repeat. Place rolls on an ungreased cookie sheet, 3 inches apart. Bake at 350°F for 23 to 25 minutes. Cool about 15 minutes. Cut logs diagonally into ½-inch slices. Arrange on cookie sheet. Bake at 300°F for 14 to 18 minutes, turning once, until golden on both sides. Melt chocolate chips and 1 tsp shortening over low heat, stirring well. Do the same with vanilla chips and remaining shortening. Drizzle mixtures over cooled biscotti. Makes about 3 dozen biscotti.

Almond Spice Rugelach

2 cups flour
3 tbsp sugar
¼ tsp salt

1 cup butter or margarine
2 (3-ounce) packages cream cheese
⅓ cup sour cream

FILLING
¾ cup blanched almonds,
   finely chopped
⅓ cup sugar

1 tbsp butter or margarine, softened
1 tsp cinnamon
½ tsp nutmeg

GLAZE
1 egg white, beaten

nutmeg, if desired

Stir together flour, sugar, and salt. Cut in butter until mixture is crumbly. Cut in cream cheese. Stir in sour cream to form a soft dough. Shape dough into a ball. Cover and refrigerate for at least 4 hours. Remove from refrigerator and let sit at room temperature for about 15 minutes. Divide dough into 4 pieces and shape each piece into a ball. Place each ball on a floured surface and flatten slightly, then roll each into a circle about 1/8 inch thick. Mix together all filling ingredients and sprinkle 1/4 cup of mixture onto each circle. Cut circles into 12 wedges each and roll up wedges starting from the wide end. Place rolled wedges on an ungreased cookie sheet, 1 inch apart, and shape into crescents. Brush with beaten egg white and sprinkle with nutmeg. Bake at 350°F for 22 to 25 minutes. Makes about 4 dozen cookies.

Chocolate Mint Pinwheels

½ cup sugar
½ cup butter or margarine,
 softened
1 egg
1 tsp vanilla
1 (1-ounce) square unsweetened baking chocolate, melted,
 then cooled
2 to 3 drops green food coloring

¼ tsp peppermint extract
1 ½ cups flour
½ tsp baking powder
¼ tsp salt

Beat together sugar, butter, egg, vanilla, and peppermint extract at medium speed until creamy. Reduce speed and beat in flour, baking powder, and salt. Remove half the dough and add melted chocolate to remaining half, mixing well. Beat green food coloring into first half. Wrap both halves in plastic wrap and refrigerate for 1 hour. Roll out chocolate dough between two sheets of floured waxed paper, forming dough into a 12 x 7-inch rectangle. Do the same with the green dough. Remove waxed paper and place green dough on top of the chocolate, pressing them together slightly. Roll them up together from the 12-inch side. Wrap dough in plastic wrap and refrigerate 2 hours. Cut roll into slices, ¼ inch thick, and place on an ungreased cookie sheet, 1 inch apart. Bake at 375°F for 7 to 9 minutes. Makes about 4 dozen cookies.

Lemon Frosted Ginger Cookies

½ cup sugar
½ cup butter or margarine, softened
1 egg
½ cup light molasses
½ cup hot water

2 ⅓ cups flour
1 tsp baking soda
1 tsp ginger
½ tsp cinnamon
¼ tsp salt
¼ tsp cloves

FROSTING
2 cups powdered sugar
¼ cup butter or margarine, softened
grated lemon peel, if desired

2 tsp grated lemon peel
2 to 3 tbsp milk

Beat together sugar, butter, and egg at medium speed until creamy. Reduce speed and add molasses and water. Beat in all remaining cookie ingredients. Drop dough onto a greased cookie sheet by rounded teaspoons, 2 inches apart. Bake at 375°F for 8 to 10 minutes. Mix powdered sugar, butter, and lemon peel, adding enough milk for desired frosting consistency. Frost cooled cookies. If desired, sprinkle with grated lemon peel. Makes about 4 dozen cookies.

Cashew Butter Cookies

½ cup packed brown sugar
¾ cup butter or margarine,
  softened
½ cup honey
1 egg

2 cups flour
¾ tsp baking soda
½ tsp baking powder
1 cup salted cashews, chopped
salted cashew halves

Mix brown sugar, butter, honey, and egg at medium speed until creamy. Reduce speed and add all remaining ingredients except cashews. Stir in chopped cashews by hand. Drop dough onto an ungreased cookie sheet by rounded teaspoons, 2 inches apart. Place a cashew half on top of each cookie. Bake at 375°F for 6 to 9 minutes. Makes about 4 ½ dozen cookies.

Buttery Cutout Cookies

1 cup butter or margarine, softened
1 (3-ounce) package cream cheese, softened
¾ cup sugar

1 egg
1 tsp vanilla
3 cups flour

At medium speed, beat together all ingredients except flour. Reduce speed and mix in flour. Divide dough into two parts and wrap each in plastic wrap. Refrigerate for at least 2 hours. Roll out dough, one half at a time, on a floured surface. When dough is ¼ inch thick, cut with 2 ½-inch cookie cutters. Place cookies on an ungreased cookie sheet, 1 inch apart. Bake at 375°F for 7 to 10 minutes. Makes about 3 ½ dozen cookies.

Peppermint Sandwich Cookies

1 cup sugar
1 cup butter or margarine,
   softened
1 egg
1 tsp vanilla
½ cup peppermint or spearmint candy, crushed

2 cups flour
½ cup cocoa
½ tsp baking soda
¼ tsp salt

FROSTING
2 cups powdered sugar
¼ cup butter or margarine, softened
½ tsp peppermint extract
2 to 3 tbsp milk
¼ cup peppermint or spearmint candy, crushed

Beat together sugar, butter, egg, and vanilla at medium speed. Reduce speed and mix in flour, cocoa, baking soda, and salt. Stir in crushed candy by hand. Divide dough in half. Shape each half into a ball and flatten to about ½ inch. Wrap each part in plastic wrap and refrigerate for 1 to 2 hours. Roll out dough, half at a time, on a floured surface. When dough is ⅛ inch thick, cut it with 1-inch cookie cutters and place on a cookie sheet, 1 inch apart. Bake at 400°F for 6 to 8 minutes. Mix powdered sugar, butter, and peppermint extract, adding enough milk for desired consistency. Stir in crushed candy by hand. When cookies have cooled completely, spread ½ tsp of frosting on half the cookies. Place the remaining cookies on top of the frosted cookies and press together slightly. Makes about 6 dozen cookies.

Spumoni Slices

1 cup sugar
1 cup butter or margarine,
   softened
1 egg

1 tsp vanilla
2 ½ cups flour
¼ tsp baking powder
¼ tsp salt

¼ cup well-drained maraschino cherries, finely chopped
2 to 3 drops red food coloring
¼ cup pistachio nuts, finely chopped
2 to 3 drops green food coloring

Mix sugar, butter, egg, and vanilla at medium speed until creamy. Reduce speed and beat in flour, baking powder, and salt. Divide the dough into three equal parts. Mix cherries and red food coloring into one third by hand. Into a second third, mix pistachios and green food coloring by hand. Place each third between two sheets of waxed paper and roll into 7 x 6-inch rectangles. Remove waxed paper and layer pink, white, and green dough. Wrap in plastic wrap and refrigerate for 2 hours, or overnight. Cut dough into three 7 x 2-inch rectangles. Cut rectangles into ¼-inch slices and place on an ungreased cookie sheet, 1 inch apart. Bake at 350°F for 9 to 11 minutes. Makes about 7 dozen cookies.

Almond Brickle Sugar Cookies

2 ¼ cups flour
1 cup sugar
1 cup butter or margarine,
    softened

1 egg
1 tsp baking soda
1 tsp vanilla
1 (6-ounce) package
    toffee chips

Mix together all ingredients except toffee chips at medium speed. Stir in toffee chips by hand. Form dough into 1-inch balls and place on an ungreased cookie sheet, 2 inches apart. Bake at 350°F for 8 to 11 minutes. Makes about 4 dozen cookies.

Chocolate Cinnamon Tea Cakes

¾ cup packed brown sugar
¾ cup butter or margarine, softened
2 (1-ounce) squares unsweetened baking chocolate,
    melted, then cooled
1 tsp vanilla   ½ tsp cinnamon
2 cups flour   powdered sugar
½ tsp salt

At medium speed, beat brown sugar and butter until creamy. Beat in chocolate and vanilla. Reduce speed and add flour, salt, and cinnamon. Form dough into 1-inch balls and place on an ungreased cookie sheet, 2 inches apart. Bake at 350°F for 8 to 10 minutes. While still warm, roll cookies in powdered sugar. Repeat when cool. Makes about 4 dozen cookies.

Chewy Gumdrop Bars

1 ½ cups packed brown sugar
¼ cup butter or margarine,
   softened
4 eggs
2 cups flour
1 tsp cinnamon
¼ tsp cloves

¼ tsp nutmeg
¼ tsp salt
1 cup walnuts, chopped
1 cup (6 ounces) gumdrops,
   cut up
powdered sugar

Mix together brown sugar and butter at medium speed until creamy. Beat in eggs. Reduce speed and add flour, cinnamon, cloves, nutmeg, and salt. Stir in walnuts and gumdrops by hand. Spread into a greased 13 x 9-inch pan. Bake at 350°F for 30 minutes. Cool 30 minutes, then cut into bars and roll in powdered sugar. Makes about 48 bars.

Orange Butter Cream Squares

CRUST
1 ¼ cups chocolate wafer cookies, finely crushed (about 25)

⅓ cup butter or margarine, softened

FILLING
1 ½ cups powdered sugar
⅓ cup butter or margarine
2 tsp grated orange peel

1 tbsp milk
½ tsp vanilla

GLAZE
1 tbsp butter or margarine, melted   1 tbsp cocoa

Stir together all crust ingredients and press into the bottom of an ungreased 9-inch square pan. Cover and refrigerate for about 1 hour. Beat all filling ingredients at medium speed until creamy. Spread over crust.

Mix glaze ingredients and drizzle over filling. Refrigerate for 1 to 2 hours, until firm. Store in refrigerator. Makes about 25 bars.

Strawberry Linzer Bars

1 ¾ cups flour
½ cup sugar
1 (2-ounce) package hazelnuts
   or blanched almonds,
   ground (½ cup)
1 tsp grated lemon peel
½ tsp cinnamon
½ tsp baking powder
¼ tsp salt

½ cup butter or margarine,
   cut into pieces
1 egg, beaten
1 tsp vanilla
½ cup seedless strawberry
   or raspberry jam
powdered sugar
cinnamon

Mix flour, sugar, hazelnuts, lemon peel, cinnamon, baking powder, and salt. Add butter and beat at low speed until crumbly. Beat in egg and vanilla. Divide dough in half. Press half the dough into an ungreased 9-inch square pan. Spread jam on dough to within ½ inch of the edge. Roll out other half of dough between two sheets of floured waxed paper, forming an 11 x 10-inch rectangle. Remove waxed paper and cut dough into twenty ½-inch strips. Place strips over jam diagonally, forming a lattice crust. Bake at 350°F for 23 to 28 minutes. When cool, sprinkle with powdered sugar and cinnamon. Store in the refrigerator. Makes about 36 bars.

Chocolate-Covered Raisin Drops

1 cup packed brown sugar
½ cup butter or margarine, softened
1 cup sour cream
2 eggs
2 tsp vanilla
2 ¼ cups flour

1 tsp baking soda
½ tsp salt
1 (10-ounce) package semisweet chocolate-covered raisins (1 ⅓ cups)
½ cup nuts, chopped, if desired

Beat together brown sugar and butter at medium speed until creamy. Beat in sour cream, eggs, and vanilla. Reduce speed and add flour, baking soda, and salt. Stir in chocolate-covered raisins and nuts by hand. Drop dough onto an ungreased cookie sheet by rounded teaspoons, 2 inches apart. Bake at 350°F for 9 to 11 minutes. Makes about 5 dozen cookies.

Chocolate Drizzled Lime Cookies

2 ¾ cups flour
1 ½ cups sugar
1 cup butter or margarine,
    softened
¾ cup flaked coconut
2 eggs

1 tbsp grated lime peel
3 tbsp lime juice
1 ½ tsp cream of tartar
1 tsp baking soda
¼ tsp salt

DRIZZLE
½ cup semisweet chocolate chips

2 tbsp shortening

Beat together all cookie ingredients at low speed. Drop dough onto an ungreased cookie sheet by rounded teaspoons, 2 inches apart. Bake at 400°F for 7 to 10 minutes. Melt chocolate chips and shortening over medium heat, stirring until smooth. When cookies are completely cool, drizzle them with chocolate. Makes about 4 dozen cookies.

Cherry Pecan Slices

1 cup butter or margarine, softened
½ cup sugar
½ cup powdered sugar
1 egg
1 tsp vanilla
2 ¼ cups flour
1 ½ cups red and/or green candied cherries,
    halved
1 tbsp flour
1 cup pecans, coarsely chopped

At medium speed, mix butter, sugar, powdered sugar, egg, and vanilla. Reduce speed and add 2 ¼ cups flour. Roll cherries in 1 tbsp flour and stir cherries and pecans into dough by hand. Cover and refrigerate for 1 hour. On floured surface, shape dough into three 1-inch thick rolls. Wrap rolls in plastic wrap and refrigerate 3 hours, or overnight. Cut rolls into ¼-inch slices and place on an ungreased cookie sheet, 1 inch apart. Bake at 350°F for 11 to 13 minutes. Makes about 10 dozen cookies.

Twinkling Anise Stars

1 cup sugar
1 cup butter or margarine,
  softened
1 egg
1 tsp anise extract

1 tsp vanilla
2 ½ cups flour
½ tsp baking powder
¼ tsp salt
decorator sugars

Beat sugar, butter, egg, anise extract, and vanilla at medium speed until creamy. Reduce speed and beat in flour, baking powder, and salt. Divide the dough into two parts. Wrap each part in plastic wrap and refrigerate for 1 to 2 hours. Roll out dough on a floured surface, one half at a time, until it is $1/8$ inch thick. Cut with 2-inch star cookie cutters and place cookies on an ungreased cookie sheet, 1 inch apart. Sprinkle cookies with decorator sugars. Bake at 375°F for 5 to 7 minutes. Makes about 5 dozen cookies.

Black Walnut Macaroons

2 egg whites
1 tsp vanilla
½ cup sugar
2 ½ cups flaked coconut

1 (2-ounce) package chopped
black walnuts (½ cup)
2 tbsp flour

Beat egg whites and vanilla at high speed until foamy. Gradually add sugar while beating until soft peaks form. Gently stir in coconut, walnuts, and flour by hand. Drop dough onto lined cookie sheets by rounded teaspoons, 2 inches apart. Bake at 300°F for 18 to 22 minutes. Makes about 3 dozen cookies.

Apricot Nut Cookies

1 ½ cups powdered sugar
1 cup butter or margarine,
    softened
1 egg
½ tsp vanilla
1 (6-ounce) package chopped,
    dried apricots, less ⅓ cup
powdered sugar

2 cups flour
1 tsp baking soda
1 tsp cream of tartar
1 cup coarsely chopped
    pecans, toasted

At medium speed, beat powdered sugar and butter. Beat in egg and vanilla. Reduce speed and add flour, baking soda, and cream of tartar. Stir in pecans and apricots by hand. Drop dough onto an ungreased cookie sheet by rounded teaspoons, 2 inches apart. Bake at 350°F for 11 to 15 minutes. While still warm, sprinkle with powdered sugar. Repeat when cool. Makes about 6 dozen cookies.

Honey 'N Spice Cookies

2 cups flour
¾ cup sugar
¾ cup butter or margarine,
   softened
¼ cup honey
1 egg

½ tsp salt
½ tsp baking soda
½ tsp nutmeg
¼ tsp cloves
½ tsp vanilla

GLAZE
1 cup powdered sugar
2 tbsp milk

2 tsp grated orange peel

Beat together all cookie ingredients at low speed until well mixed. Cover and refrigerate for 1 to 2 hours. Drop dough onto an ungreased cookie sheet by rounded teaspoons, 2 inches apart. Bake at 375°F for 7 to 10 minutes. Mix glaze ingredients. Glaze cookies while still warm. Makes about 3 dozen cookies.

Rain Forest Gems

1 cup packed brown sugar
½ cup butter or margarine, softened
1 (8-ounce) can crushed pineapple in juice (½ cup),
   drain and keep juice
1 egg
1 tsp rum-flavored extract
1 ¾ cups flour
1 tsp baking powder
1 tsp baking soda
¼ tsp salt
½ cup flaked coconut
1 (2-ounce) package Brazil nuts, coarsely chopped (½ cup)

FROSTING
2 cups powdered sugar
¼ cup butter or margarine, melted
1 tsp vanilla
2 to 3 tbsp pineapple juice
toasted coconut, if desired

At medium speed, beat together brown sugar and butter. Beat in pineapple, egg, and rum-flavored extract. Reduce speed and add flour, baking powder, baking soda, and salt. Stir in coconut and nuts by hand. Drop dough onto a greased cookie sheet by rounded teaspoons, 2 inches apart. Bake at 375°F for 10 to 12 minutes.

Mix powdered sugar, butter, and vanilla at low speed, adding enough pineapple juice for desired consistency. Frost cooled cookies. If desired, sprinkle with toasted coconut. Makes about 3 ½ dozen cookies.

Snickerdoodle Pan Cookies

¾ cup sugar
¾ cup butter or margarine,
   softened
1 egg
1 tsp vanilla

1 ½ cups flour
½ tsp cream of tartar
½ tsp cinnamon
¼ tsp salt
¼ tsp baking soda

TOPPING
1 tbsp sugar
½ cup nuts, finely chopped

1 tsp cinnamon

At medium speed, beat together sugar, butter, egg, and vanilla until creamy. Reduce speed and mix in flour, cream of tartar, cinnamon, salt, and baking soda. Spread batter into a greased 15 x 10 x 1-inch jelly roll pan. Combine topping ingredients and sprinkle onto batter. Bake at 375°F for 11 to 13 minutes. Cut into 2-inch squares; cut squares diagonally into triangles. Makes about 3 dozen bars.

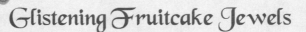

Glistening Fruitcake Jewels

CRUMB MIXTURE
2 cups flour
¾ cup butter or margarine, softened
½ cup sugar

FILLING
½ cup sugar
½ cup raisins
¼ cup orange or lemon juice
1 (8-ounce) package chopped dates
1 (2 ½-ounce) package sliced almonds
1 egg
¼ cup candied cherries, chopped

GLAZE
¾ cup powdered sugar
1 tbsp milk
½ tsp vanilla

Beat all ingredients for crumb mixture on low speed until crumbly. Press into the bottom of a greased 13 x 9-inch pan. Bake at 350°F for 15 to 20 minutes. Combine all filling ingredients except cherries. Spread over hot crust and sprinkle with cherries. Bake for 17 to 20 minutes. Mix glaze ingredients and drizzle over cooled bars. Makes about 36 bars.

Butter Almond Crisps

2 cups flour
1 cup sugar
1 cup butter or margarine,
  softened

1 egg, separated
½ tsp cinnamon
½ tsp salt

TOPPING
1 cup sliced almonds
½ tsp cinnamon

2 tbsp sugar

At low speed, beat flour, sugar, butter, egg yolk, cinnamon, and salt until well mixed. Divide dough in half. Press each half to ¹/₁₆ inch thick on a cookie sheet. Beat egg white with a fork until foamy. Brush egg white over dough and sprinkle with sliced almonds. Combine other topping ingredients and sprinkle over almonds. Bake at 350°F for 12 to 15 minutes. Cut into 2-inch squares or diamonds immediately. Makes about 42 bars.

Teatime Sandwich Cookies

2 cups flour
1 cup butter or margarine, softened
⅓ cup whipping cream

SUGAR FILLING
¾ cup powdered sugar
¼ cup butter or margarine, softened
1 tsp vanilla or almond extract
1 to 3 tsp milk
food coloring, if desired

Mix flour, butter, and whipping cream at low speed. Divide dough into three equal parts and wrap each in plastic wrap. Refrigerate for at least 2 hours. Roll out dough to $1/8$ inch thick, one portion at a time. Cut dough with 1 ½-inch round cookie cutter. Dip both sides of cookies in sugar. Place on an ungreased cookie sheet, 1 inch apart, and pierce all over with a fork. Bake at 375°F for 6 to 9 minutes.

Mix all filling ingredients except milk and food coloring, beating at medium speed. Add enough milk for desired consistency. Add food coloring if desired. When cookies are completely cool, press them together in pairs with ½ tsp of filling between pairs. Makes about 4 ½ dozen cookies.

Cranberry Apricot Tartlets

TARTLET SHELLS

¼ cup sugar
½ cup butter or margarine,
   cut into 4 pieces
1 ⅓ cups flour

¼ tsp salt
½ tsp grated orange peel
1 to 3 tbsp orange juice

FILLING

1 ½ cups fresh or
   frozen cranberries
¾ cup dried apricots,
   chopped
sweetened whipped cream, if desired

1 cup sugar
½ tsp grated orange peel
⅓ cup orange juice
¼ cup water

Combine sugar, butter, flour, and salt, beating at low speed until crumbly. Add orange peel and enough orange juice to form a dough. Divide dough into 30 equal pieces. Press dough onto the bottom and sides of greased and sugared mini-muffin cups. Bake at 375°F for 14 to 18 minutes. Loosen edges with a knife and remove shells.

Combine all filling ingredients except whipped cream, cooking over medium-high heat until mixture comes to a full boil. Stir occasionally. Reduce heat to low and cook for 15 to 20 minutes, stirring occasionally, until mixture is thickened. When filling is completely cooled, just before serving, spoon filling into shells. If desired, top with whipped cream. Makes 30 tartlets.

Moravian Christmas Cookies

4 cups flour
1 tsp ginger
1 tsp cinnamon
1 tsp mace
½ tsp cloves
¼ cup butter or margarine

¼ cup shortening
½ cup packed brown sugar
1 cup molasses
1 ½ tsp baking soda
1 tbsp very hot water

Beat together butter, shortening, and sugar until fluffy. Beat in molasses. Mix together flour and spices and add about ¼ of them to mixture. Dissolve baking soda in water and mix in. Add remaining dry ingredients a little at a time. Wrap dough and refrigerate for 4 to 6 hours. Roll out dough as thin as possible ($^1/_8$ to $^1/_{16}$ inch thick). Cut with cookie cutters and place on a greased cookie sheet, 1 ½ inches apart. Bake at 350°F for 8 minutes. Makes about 4 ½ dozen cookies.

Pfeffernüsse

German Peppernuts

3 cups flour	¼ tsp white pepper
1 tsp cinnamon	3 eggs
⅛ tsp cloves	1 cup sugar

⅓ cup blanched almonds, finely chopped
⅓ cup candied orange peel and citron, finely chopped
vanilla sugar or powdered sugar, if desired

Beat eggs, then gradually add sugar while continuing to beat. Mix flour and spices together and add to egg mixture. Mix in almonds and orange peel. Wrap dough in foil and refrigerate 2 to 3 days. Roll out dough, a little at a time to ¼ to ½ inch thick. Cut dough with 1 ¾-inch round cookie cutter and place on a greased cookie sheet, 1 inch apart. Bake at 350°F for 15 to 18 minutes. Before eating, store in a covered container for 1 to 2 weeks with half an apple. Before serving, roll in sugar. Makes about 3 ½ dozen cookies.

Lebkuchen

3 cups flour
1 tsp cinnamon
½ tsp cloves
1 cup honey
1 tsp finely grated lemon rind
½ cup blanched almonds, finely chopped
½ cup mixed candied orange peel and citron, finely chopped

½ tsp baking soda
½ tsp nutmeg
1 cup packed brown sugar
1 egg
1 tbsp lemon juice

FROSTING
1 cup powdered sugar

4 to 5 tsp milk

DECORATION
Blanched almonds, halved
Candied cherries, sliced or halved

Beat together sugar, honey, and egg. Mix in lemon rind and lemon juice. Combine flour, baking soda, and spices and add to egg mixture, stirring until just mixed. Stir in almonds and fruit peel. Wrap dough and refrigerate for 12 hours. Roll out dough, a piece at a time, ¼ inch thick. Cut with a round cookie cutter or cut into 2 ½ x 1 ½-inch rectangles. Place cookies on a greased cookie sheet, 2 inches apart. Bake at 400°F for 8 minutes. Beat frosting ingredients until smooth and spread on top of cooled cookies. Decorate with almonds and cherries. Makes about 4 ½ dozen.

Don't let cookie baking become a chore. If you're alone, listen to Christmas music while you bake, spending time in prayer and worship. Or to make baking go more quickly, get together with a friend and share your lives with each other while you work.

Other
Christmas
Desserts

Bûche de Noël

Yule Log Cake

1 cup flour
1 ¼ tsp baking powder
¼ tsp salt
1 tbsp cocoa

4 eggs
⅔ cup sugar
1 tbsp hot water

FILLING

½ cup butter or margarine
2 ¼ cups powdered sugar

2 tbsp cocoa
2 to 3 tbsp milk

Sift together flour, baking powder, salt, and cocoa. In a bowl over a pan of hot water, whisk together sugar and eggs until pale and thick. Remove from heat and fold in half the flour mixture. Fold in remaining flour mixture, along with hot water. Pour batter into a lined jelly roll pan. Bake at 425°F for about 10 minutes. Turn cake onto a sheet of waxed paper and trim edges of cake. Before it cools, roll up cake with the paper inside. Set aside to cool. For filling, mix butter and powdered sugar. Beat in cocoa and milk until mixture is fluffy. Unroll cake and remove paper. Spread ¼ of filling on cake and roll it up. Spread the rest of the filling on the outside of the log. Use a fork to make swirls and ridges like tree bark. Decorate with powdered sugar, if desired.

Pán de Pascua

Christmas Cake

1 cup butter or margarine
2 cups powdered sugar
1 cup seedless raisins
1 ⅓ cups mixed crystallized fruits, chopped
4 ¾ cups flour
2 to 3 whole cloves
1 tbsp vinegar

1 ½ tbsp warm water
6 eggs, separated
½ cup walnuts, broken
2 tbsp baking powder
1 tsp cinnamon
¼ tsp nutmeg
2 tbsp rum flavoring
1 cup milk

Beat butter and warm water until fluffy. Add powdered sugar a little at a time. Beat in egg yolks. Mix in raisins, candied fruits, and walnuts by hand. Stir in flour, baking powder, spices, rum flavoring, and vinegar. Beat egg whites until they form soft peaks, then fold them into the batter. Add enough of the milk so that the batter drops from a spoon, but is not too soft. Pour batter into a greased and lined 8-inch round pan. Bake at 375°F for 15 minutes. Lower temperature to 325°F and bake for 50 to 55 minutes. Cool for 10 minutes, then remove cake from pan to cool. Sprinkle with powdered sugar before serving.

Puff Pastry

4 cups flour
1 tsp salt
1 tbsp lemon juice

12 to 14 tbsp ice water
1 ¾ cups butter or margarine
¼ cup shortening

Mix flour and salt on a pastry board. Make a well in the center and add lemon juice and 6 tbsp water. Stir with fingers, mixing in flour. Gradually add more water until flour is all absorbed and dough forms a ball. Knead lightly. Wrap in waxed paper and a damp cloth. Refrigerate 30 minutes. Mix butter and shortening with a spatula. Form into a brick, wrap in waxed paper, and refrigerate. Roll out dough on floured surface, forming a 12-inch circle. Place butter on dough and fold dough around it, sealing edges. Roll into a 16 x 8-inch rectangle, short side facing you. Fold dough into thirds, sealing edges. Wrap in waxed paper and a damp cloth. Refrigerate 15 minutes. Short side facing you, roll out dough to similar size and repeat procedure. Repeat 8 more times. Wrap pastry and refrigerate overnight. Use as directed. Pastry will keep several days.

Kerstkrans

Christmas Ring

1 ⅓ cups almonds, ground
½ cup sugar
grated rind of 1 lemon

pinch of salt
2 eggs
½ pound prepared
   puff pastry

DECORATIONS
2 tbsp apricot jam
candied cherries, halved

candied citron or angelica
toasted almond flakes

For filling, mix ground almonds and sugar. Stir in lemon rind and salt. Beat 1 egg, then add to mixture. On floured surface, roll the almond paste into 1-inch-thick pieces. Wrap pieces in waxed paper and refrigerate until cold. Roll out pastry on floured surface, making a strip 3 ½ inches wide and ⅛ inch thick. Put almond paste rolls end to end on strip. Moisten one edge of the pastry with water and fold dough over the paste. Seal the seam with your fingertips. Shape filled pastry roll into a ring, seam side down, and place on a floured cookie sheet. Join the ends securely. Beat other egg together with a little water. Brush egg mixture over pastry ring. Bake at 425°F for 30 minutes.

Heat apricot jam with 1 or 2 tbsp water and glaze ring before pastry cools. Decorate with cherries, candied citron, and almond flakes.

Buñuelos Navideños

Christmas Fritters

2 cups water
¼ tsp salt
2 tbsp butter or margarine
4 tbsp cornmeal

¾ cup flour
5 eggs
(oil for frying)

SYRUP
1 cup sugar
1 cup water
4-inch cinnamon stick

1 tsp lemon juice
1 tsp orange flower water

Boil water, salt, and butter. Add cornmeal and flour and stir over low heat until mixture forms a ball. Put dough in a bowl and beat it with a wooden spoon until it cools. Beat in eggs one at a time. Heat oil to 375°F in deep fryer. Drop tablespoons of dough into oil a few at a time. Remove when golden and drain on paper towels. For the syrup, heat sugar and water in saucepan together with the cinnamon stick. After sugar dissolves, boil syrup until it thickens slightly. Turn off heat and remove cinnamon stick. Stir in lemon juice and orange flower water. Arrange fritters on a plate and pour syrup over them.

Klenäter

Christmas Crullers

4 egg yolks
¼ cup sugar
1 ½ cups flour
3 tbsp butter or margarine

1 tbsp brandy
1 tbsp grated lemon rind
shortening (for frying)
½ cup sugar

Cut butter into small pieces over flour. Mix with pastry blender until crumbly. Beat together egg yolks and sugar and add mixture to flour and butter. Mix in brandy and lemon rind. Shape dough into a ball, wrap in waxed paper, and refrigerate. Roll dough out thinly on a floured surface. Cut dough into strips 3 inches long and ¾ inches wide. Make a cut in the center of each strip and pull one end through the hole. Heat shortening to 375°F in deep fryer. Fry crullers, a few at a time, until golden. Drain on paper towels and sprinkle with sugar.

Plum Pudding

1 ½ cups seedless raisins
½ cup dried currants
½ cup mixed candied fruit, finely chopped
1 tart apple, peeled, cored, and finely grated
finely grated rind of 1 lemon
finely grated rind of 1 orange

¾ cup orange juice

1 cup flour

1 tsp baking powder

½ tsp salt

1 tsp cinnamon

½ tsp allspice

¼ tsp nutmeg

1 cup packed brown sugar

⅓ cup molasses

1 cup finely ground suet

3 eggs, lightly beaten

½ cup blanched almonds, minced, toasted

Mix fruits, rinds, and orange juice and let sit 30 minutes. Mix in remaining ingredients. Pour batter into 2 greased 1-quart molds or metal bowls and cover with a double thickness of foil, making sure foil is secured in place. Set molds on a rack in a large kettle and add enough boiling water so the water level is halfway up the sides of the pudding molds. Cover the kettle and steam for 4 hours, adding boiling water occasionally to maintain water level. Leave puddings on rack until cool, then refrigerate. To reheat, steam 1 hour as they were cooked. Remove puddings from molds onto a hot platter. Serve with Hard Sauce.

Hard Sauce

½ cup butter or margarine, softened
2 cups powdered sugar
⅛ tsp salt
1 tbsp hot water
1 tsp vanilla

Beat butter until creamy, then gradually add sugar. Beat in remaining ingredients until fluffy. Serve chilled or at room temperature.

Berliner Pfannkuchen

½ package active dried yeast
5 ounces warm milk
4 cups flour
¼ cup butter or margarine,
  melted

2 eggs
pinch of salt
¾ cup plum or apricot jam
shortening (for frying)
½ cup sugar

Sprinkle yeast onto warm milk. Whisk and leave in a warm place until yeast has dissolved and mixture is bubbling. Mix in 1 cup of flour and leave to rise in a warm place for 1 hour. Beat in butter, eggs, salt, and the rest of the flour, forming a smooth dough. Cover and put in a warm place until the dough has doubled in size. Roll out dough thinly on a floured surface. Cut with circular cookie cutter or the top of a glass. Put 1 tbsp jam on half the circles and place the rest of the circles on top of the jam. Press edges together. Cover and let rise in a warm place.

Heat shortening to 375°F in deep fryer. Fry doughnuts a few at a time for about 4 minutes, turning over when half done. Drain on paper towels and roll in sugar.

Edinburgh Gingerbread

4 cups flour
¼ tsp salt
1 ½ tsp ginger
1 ½ tsp cinnamon
1 ½ tsp mixed spice
½ tsp cloves
1 cup pitted dates,
   chopped coarsely

1 cup walnuts,
   chopped coarsely
1 cup butter or margarine
1 cup molasses
1 cup packed brown sugar
4 eggs, beaten
1 tsp baking soda
1 to 2 tbsp warm milk

Mix together flour, salt, spices, dates, and walnuts. Melt butter, molasses, and sugar over low heat. Pour mixture gradually over flour mixture, stirring well. Beat in eggs. Dissolve baking soda in warm milk and add to mixture. Stir well with a wooden spoon, adding more milk if dough is too stiff. Pour batter into a greased and lined 8-inch square pan. Bake at 350°F for 20 minutes. Lower temperature to 300°F and bake for another 2 hours.

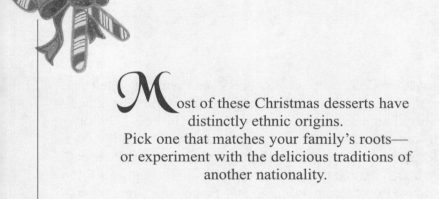

$\mathcal{M}$ost of these Christmas desserts have
distinctly ethnic origins.
Pick one that matches your family's roots—
or experiment with the delicious traditions of
another nationality.

Traditional
Christmas
Beverages

Eggnog

4 eggs, separated
1/2 cup sugar
2 cups cold milk
1 cup cold light cream

1 1/2 tsp vanilla
1/8 tsp salt
1/4 tsp nutmeg

Beat egg yolks together with $1/4$ cup sugar until thick. Gradually mix in milk, cream, vanilla, salt, and $1/8$ tsp nutmeg, beating until frothy. Beat egg whites with remaining sugar until it forms soft peaks, then fold into egg yolk mixture. Cover and chill. Mix well before serving and sprinkle with remaining nutmeg.

Mulled Cider

Simmer 2 quarts apple cider and 1 ½ cups sugar in a large pan. Add the following ingredients tied up in a cloth bag:

2 tsp whole allspice   2 tsp whole cloves
5 cinnamon sticks

Simmer for 20 minutes covered, then remove the spice bag and discard. Add:

4 cups cranberry juice   2 cups orange juice
1 cup lemon juice

Simmer another 15 minutes. Garnish with orange and lemon slices and serve hot.